The Blended Family Q&A

400 Questions to Spark Fun and Thought-Provoking Conversations

Jessica Ashley

ROCKRIDGE
PRESS

Interior and Cover Designer: Scott Petrower
Art Producer: Alyssa Williams
Editor: Nora Spiegel
Production Editor: Caroline Flanagan
Production Manager: Martin Worthington

All illustrations used under license from istock.com.

Paperback ISBN: 978-1-63807-288-1 | eBook ISBN: 978-1-63807-667-4
R0

Introduction

Blended families, you are in exactly the right place.

This book was created for every family that is growing and getting to know each other. It is written for blended families, which are created when two families merge, and where there might be several co-parents or stepparents, adopted children, foster children, or bonus kids. Your blended family might also include pets, stories, and experiences from other parts of your lives and in different homes. You might have your own beautiful definition for your blended family.

I believe that every family is always evolving, but that blended families are something special. We've chosen to live with and love each other, which can fill our homes with laughter and our hearts with happiness, but can also come with some distinct challenges.

This book speaks right to my own family and profession. As a certified divorce coach at Divorce Coach for Moms, and creator of the Single Mom Nation community and podcast, my calling is to empower and guide parents through tough transitions so that we can all have bigger, happier, and healthier lives. We are all experts about our own lives. That includes our children. I often ask my own kids, "What are we doing well? What could we be doing better?" Their responses are always clear, inspiring, and humbling. No matter what the path forward, we are on the road together.

Asking questions is critical. It helps us share what we feel and think, and learn to really listen. This book gives you both the questions and the chance to hear each other. For anyone who's asked their child what happened at school and heard "nothing" or "I can't remember," my hope is that these prompts will inspire more substantive responses, some giggles, and maybe even a few tears or hugs.

My second hope is that you'll feel deeply connected. If your blended family is struggling today, or has been for a while, know that millions of us are nodding compassionately and are with you in spirit as you find your way forward.

This book is designed to help you work through the complex feelings and day-to-day challenges that your family may experience and help you celebrate the loving blended family you are and that you are always becoming. While spending time asking and listening is a great strategy for merging your worlds, know that medical and mental health professionals can be wonderful resources for support, too. There's no shame in loving each other so much that you seek help when it's needed.

Press pause on your busy lives together and take some time and space to just be there as your own remarkable blended family—one question and response at a time. This will be good, I promise.

Jessica Ashley

How to Use This Book

This book has 400 questions written just for your blended family, to spark conversations and hold regular family meetings (that aren't about schedules or screen-time limits). These questions are written for many ages, experiences, and identities, and are for everyone in the family, from younger kids to teens to parents (and even grandparents!). There are blank spaces to write down your responses, if you choose.

Questions fall into five categories.

 Our Family explores your unique relationships and what you are building together.

 Memories and the Past asks about the experiences and lessons that shape who you are today.

 Goals and Dreams expands your imagination about all you hope to do and be, and the adventures you'll set out on individually and as a family.

 Thoughts, Feelings, and Values invites you to share how you see the world and yourself.

 Just for Fun drops you into entertaining scenarios and your lighter, imaginative side.

Some questions may send you into a fit of giggles, and others may call on you to consider a difficult moment. Although some questions may not relate to every family member or may need to be broken down for younger children, there is something in here for everyone. Hold compassionate space for each other so that you all feel comfortable being honest, vulnerable, supported, and supportive.

Four hundred questions may seem overwhelming, but you can choose just a few questions at a time or make a fun game out of doing 10 or 15 in an allotted time or during a car ride. However you choose to use these questions, you'll know exactly how to best use this book for your own blended family. Here are some ways to create connection.

Set a time to answer one or two questions (or more). Rituals help us all ease through change, feel secure, and have something to look forward to together. Try a weekly dinner question session, or a daily Q&A at breakfast.

Include it in your adventures! Take this book on the road during your first vacation or as you settle into your new home. Use it to mark family moments and memories.

Consider it a tool to wade through transitions. When new or uncomfortable interactions come up, take a break and some deep breaths, and ask questions that remind you that you're here for each other through it all. If talking is too much, pass the book around and write down your responses, or leave it out so you can add answers when the time is right.

Level up the Q&A! Designate a family reporter who can ask follow-up questions. Write your own bonus questions. Give each person one pass or a wild card to assign their question to someone else. Answer questions by category, page by page, or randomly. Choose a date to revisit your responses and reflect on how you have grown as a family over time.

Just like there is no one way to be a family, there is no prescribed way to enjoy this book, so long as you move through it together.

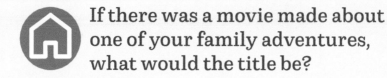 If there was a movie made about one of your family adventures, what would the title be?

 What's the best gift you've ever given to someone else? Why did you love giving it? How did they react?

If you could relive any time in your life, what would you do over? Is there a special trip or fun day you'd like to do over?

 Your family is competing in the Olympics! In which team sport will you be most likely to win a gold medal? Why would you win?

What is something new you'd like to learn this year? Why?

 What family joke or funny story will always make you laugh?

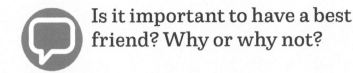 Is it important to have a best friend? Why or why not?

 When were you celebrated for something special? Why was that celebration memorable? What was the best part of that moment?

If you could explore space, where would you go? How would you get there, and what would you hope to experience?

 If you could wake up tomorrow fluent in a new language, which language would you choose and why? How would you put these new language skills to use?

If you were to choose a tattoo for one of your parents, what would it be? How do you think they would react to your choice?

 Can you be close friends with someone you know tells lies? What if your friend lies to you?

If an author is writing a biography of your life, what is one story they absolutely must include?

 If you had $5 to spend on a random act of kindness for a stranger, how would you use it? What if you had $50? Or $5,000?

What musical instrument would you like to play like a pro and why? Where would you play, and would you show off your skills to other people?

 If you could hire someone to do a household chore for you, which one would it be? How much would you be willing to pay to have it done?

If the country's president was on the phone, what advice would you give them about helping kids have great lives?

What is a family heirloom that you cherish? What treasure of your own would you one day like to pass down to younger family members?

Name game-changer! What would you call yourself if you had to choose an entirely different name? What would you rename your other family members?

 Which person outside your family gives the best advice? What advice has this person given to you?

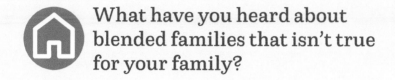 What have you heard about
blended families that isn't true
for your family?

 What is something you think is
magical? Why is it special?

Have you ever gotten in trouble for something you didn't do? What happened?

 If you suddenly became a professional athlete overnight, what would your sport be? What would you love about competing in it?

What goal or dream would you like
to make happen one day? Why?

 What is something we are doing
really well as a family?

What word makes you cringe?
What word do you say instead?

If you could be any age again,
how old would you choose to be
and why?

E-I-E-I-YOU! If you were a farmer, what would you raise on your farm and why?

 What is something you are currently avoiding doing? What's preventing you from doing it?

What do your friends call your parents? How do you address your friends' parents when you see them?

 What kind of secret keeper are you? Can you keep a secret, or do you spill it to someone else? Do you have a different way to deal with having a secret?

Has anyone ever spread a rumor about you that wasn't true? Have you ever helped spread a rumor about someone else?

 If you were invited to spend the night at any museum, which would you choose for a sleepover? How would you spend your time once it was closed to the public?

What hobby or activity always soothes your mind or calms you down? Why is it so relaxing?

 What do you know about the day you were born? What would you like to know?

What app do you use the most?
What makes the app so useful
or fun?

 What homemade gift do you
treasure? Why is it meaningful?

If you could ALWAYS win any one game, which game would you choose to be the champion of, and why?

 If you had to select a career for one of your family members, what kind of career would you choose for them? Why would it be a good career for them?

If your family had a playlist of music for your time together, what songs would you add to it? What songs would your other family members add?

 What are five things that you are grateful for right this minute?

If you could ask advice from a
family member who has passed
away or who you've never met,
which relative would you choose,
and what guidance would you
seek from them?

Imagine that you have been gifted
the power of time travel. When and
where will you transport yourself
to live for the next full year? What
will you do while you're there?

What are three things you did really well this week?

 What part of the day do you look forward to the most at home? Why is it so special to you?

What's a wonderful compliment someone has given you? Why did it feel so good to hear?

 Have you ever had an imaginary friend? Tell us all about them!

If you traveled around the world for one year, taking only a backpack with you, what five things would you absolutely have to pack, other than clothes, toiletries, and the necessities?

Do you think homework helps students to be successful? If you outlawed homework, do you think students would still be successful?

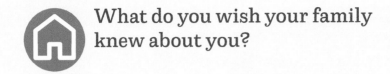

What do you wish your family knew about you?

If you could be close friends with any celebrity or famous person, who would you choose and why?

What is a story about one of your parents that you like to share? Why is it significant or fun to tell?

 It's curtain call for the school talent show! What act are you excited to perform? (Bonus points if you perform a snippet of the act right now!)

When is it okay to quit something? Have you ever quit something? Was quitting a good choice for you?

· ·

 When have you felt really proud of your family? Why does this moment stand out?

What judgment have you made about someone outside the family that turned out to be totally wrong?

What is the most difficult apology you've ever had to give to someone else?

Cha-ching! You get $1,000 to spend on your family, but you have to spend it all in 30 minutes. What do you buy, and why?

 What culture apart from your own interests you? What would you like to learn?

If you got in trouble at school, how would your parents respond? How would you feel telling them about it?

 What is something that makes you feel really safe? Why does it help you feel that way?

Have you ever chosen to stop being friends with someone? What led to your friendship breakup?

 If you discovered a new planet in the solar system, what would you call it? What significance does the name have?

How do you make big decisions?
Are there people who help you or
do you prefer to go it alone?

If you could choose anyone from
your life to live next door, who
would you pick? What would make
them a great neighbor? Who would
get your family members' votes?

What little habits are the most irritating to you? How do you handle these pet peeves? Do you have any habits of your own that irritate other people?

· ·

What is a moment when you were truly shocked or surprised? What happened?

What kind of restaurant would you like to open? What favorite food would you put on the menu first? What else would you serve?

 Look into your future! What is one thing you predict will happen in your own life? Why?

What household chore do you secretly love to do? Why do you enjoy it?

 If you had a million dollars to give to a charity or a cause that is meaningful to you, where would you donate the money and why?

Have you ever pulled a prank on someone else? How did it go? How would you react if that prank was pulled on you?

 If you were invisible for a day, where would you go and what would you do? What could be some challenges? What would be most fun about being unseen?

What's one thing you've gotten better at this year? How did you improve at this thing?

 What is your favorite thing to do at the home of a grandparent or other relative? Why?

What color is the most *you*? Why?

 What's the best party you've ever thrown or that you've been to? Why was it so fun?

If you stumbled on a group of aliens from another planet, what are the first things you'd teach them about life on Earth? What would you want to know about their lives?

 What is the worst job or chore you've ever had? Why was it so awful?

What is a special family day that you like to remember? Why was that day so memorable?

How are you different now than you were three years ago? How did you make those changes?

What is or was your most lovable stuffed animal? Why is it your favorite?

 Which carnival game or ride do you wish you had outside your family home permanently (bouncy house, dunk tank, Ferris wheel, or something else fun)?

What character from a book, movie, or show inspires you to be who you want to be, and why?

 What is a rule you don't currently have in your home but you'd like to institute? How would it help?

What is the best nickname you've ever been given? Why was it so fitting for you?

 What is your first memory?

What smell makes you cringe?
Why? How do you avoid it?

 What makes a classroom a great
place to learn? If you are no longer
in school, what makes a workplace
a great environment to thrive in
your job?

What do you call the members of your blended family? Do you use labels, like **stepdad** or **half sister** or **bonus kid**? Or have you created your own special names?

 What's your favorite photograph of you or a family member? How do you feel when you see it?

What's your favorite autumn memory? What fun activities do you look forward to every single fall?

 If you had to make everyone in your family smile, what would you do? What if you had to make everyone you know smile? What if you expanded it to everyone in the world?

If you could relocate your whole family to anywhere in the world, where would you choose to live, and why?

 What new holiday traditions would you like to start this year? What holiday traditions is it time to end, and which ones do you want to continue forever?

What's the last book you read that you wished would never end? Why was it so compelling?

 Can you recall a silly or funny dream you had recently? What was so funny about your dream?

If you could become your favorite animated character for a day, who would it be? Why?

 Have you ever saved up for something that you purchased for yourself? What was that experience like for you? What is something you would like to save up to buy for yourself in the future?

What song will get everyone in your family grooving?

· ·

 What is a dare you've taken? What did you do, and how did you feel about it?

What were you like as a baby? Are you still that way?

· ·

 If you were awarding Worst TV Show of All Time, which one would get the top prize, and why?

If you could go back in time to live
for one day as any historical figure,
who would you choose, and why?

· ·

 What snacks are always in
the cabinet at your home?
Which snacks would you like
to stock up on?

What is the best decision you've ever made? Why was it so good?

 When have you been really brave? What gave you the courage you needed in that moment?

Get ready to jam out! What are your very best dance moves? (Bonus points for showing them off right now!)

What are three places you'd love to visit? Why? They can be somewhere close or somewhere far away.

What's something your parents are really strict about? What's something they are really relaxed about?

 When have you felt completely embarrassed? How did you get over it?

What is your favorite subject or activity during school? What makes it special to you?

 You are treated to a delicious meal anywhere in the world! Where do you fly for one day just to have that meal? What do you order?

What job at an amusement park would you enjoy the most? What jobs would you hire your family members to do?

 What does it take to make a blended family work well? When does your blended family work the best together?

When can money make people happier? When can money make people feel worse?

 Who was a good friend to you today? Who were you a good friend to today?

What is one food that you will always order if it is on the menu? Why is that your go-to order?

 What's one wish you'd use to help people across the world? How would it help the people of our planet?

What things are important for your family to agree on at home? Is it house rules, politics, a favorite TV show, or something else? What topics do you disagree on that you'd like to resolve?

 How do you like to meet new friends? Where did you meet the close friends you have now?

What is something you used to be afraid of but aren't now? How did that fear disappear?

 What's the most radical change you've ever made (or would make) to your appearance? How did other people react?

Can you imagine what kind of grandparent you'd be? Even if it is decades away, what traditions would you carry on with younger family members? What would you do differently?

 When someone asks you your nationality or race, how do you respond? What do you like to share about your family's culture with other people?

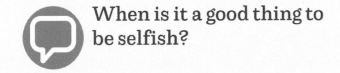 When is it a good thing to be selfish?

 When have you felt really jealous? Did you tell anyone?

What are your favorite nicknames for your family pet? If you don't have any pets at home, which animal would you choose, and what would you call it?

Which boss, teacher, or coach taught you something valuable about being a leader? What lessons did they teach you?

What team, if any, does your family cheer on together? If you are a fan family, what are some of the rituals you have?

 When was the last time you said a bad word? Why did you say it?

Have you ever walked or talked in your sleep? Have you ever witnessed someone else walk or talk in their sleep? What happened?

 What's your lucky number? How did it become so lucky?

If you were a scientist, what problem would you like to solve? Would you like to do research, conduct lab experiments, or have some other way of understanding our world and helping people?

 What's the first thing you do when you wake up in the morning? What else is going on in your home at that time?

Do you believe love at first sight exists? How would you know if you are experiencing it?

What is a story you love to hear your parent or family members tell about you? Why do you love to listen to it?

What is one song you hope to never hear again? Why would you ban it?

 What's one thing you'd like to finish in the next month? How will it feel to complete it?

Who in your family would you like to thank for helping you out recently? What did they do that was so helpful?

 What qualities make someone a great friend for you?

What is your life story (so far), told in only three sentences?

 What's the funniest joke you know?

What motto do you live by? Why are these words important to you?

 What's one question you've wanted to ask one of your parents for a long time? What's a question you think they'd like to ask you?

What's the least helpful advice someone older has given you? Did you take it?

 What's the best costume you've ever worn? What made it great?

Which actor should play you in the movie about your life? Who should play your parents?

 What hobbies would you love to turn into a job or business?

What cooking or baking traditions does your family have that you love? What do those traditions remind you of or connect you to?

 If you were someone else, would you be friends with yourself? Why?

What lullaby or bedtime ritual was soothing to you when you were younger? Does it still comfort you now?

 If you could have a conversation with any animal, which would you like to talk to, and what would you like to learn or share?

Ocean, river, stream, pool, or puddle—which would you most like to spend the day splashing around in?

 What do you discuss during family meetings? If you called a family meeting, what would you want to talk about together?

What is your favorite way to relax?
How do the other people in your
family relax?

 If you could change anything about
your childhood, what would you
revise? Why?

Imagine that you are designing the world's most incredible amusement park. What dream roller coaster or ride will you build? Why will it be such a thrill or so much fun? How do you hope people react when they ride on it?

 Have you ever turned down an opportunity even though you really wanted to say yes? Do you ever wonder what it'd be like now if you'd answered differently?

Which types of food does your family know you will not eat? Which food does each of your other family members hate?

 In what ways are you strong?

What is a game or activity that will always remind you of being a kid? Who did you play it with and what stories does it evoke?

 What song could you listen to over and over and still enjoy? Why is it so good, even on repeat?

How might our world change if kids were the leaders? Who would you vote for if children were in charge?

 What is one thing your family needs to really enjoy your time together? Is this a feeling (like love or compassion), an activity (like playing miniature golf or laughing), or something tangible (like pizza or a cozy couch)?

What sport or activity has changed you for the better? What has it given you?

 What is the last kind thing you did for someone else?

What's the weirdest sandwich you've ever created? How did it rate on a deliciousness scale of awful to awesome? Who in your family is most likely to taste your creation?

What did you learn in school that helps you in your daily life? What's something you learned that you never use now?

What's something hard that has happened in your life that actually helped you feel closer to the people you love? How did it connect you?

 What is something you're really confident about, and how do you share that with other people?

If you had a pen pal who lived in another country, what is the first thing you would share about your life? What would you want to know first about your new friend?

 What is the one outfit you'd keep if you had to get rid of the rest of your clothes? Why would you choose that look?

What's something really wonderful or fulfilling that you did during the COVID-19 pandemic? How did it change your experience of that time?

 When has a family member surprised you—in a good way?

Who is a trusted adult outside of the family—maybe a teacher, friend, or aunt—who you feel comfortable calling if you need help? Why do you choose them?

What TV theme song or opening credits do you still remember from a show you watched when you were younger? Why has it stuck with you? (Extra points if you perform it for your family!)

If you were a mad scientist, what would you invent to make your life even more exciting?

 What is something you really want but are a little nervous to say aloud? Why are you hesitant to share?

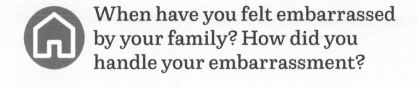 When have you felt embarrassed by your family? How did you handle your embarrassment?

 What's a crazy coincidence you've experienced (or you've heard happened to someone else)?

When have you had stage fright? How did you handle it?

 Which social media star or influencer would you like to invite you to guest host on their channel or platform? What would you talk about or post? Why is this your dream takeover?

Has anyone ever discouraged you from pursuing your dreams? How did you respond?

 Which families are great role models? How do they inspire you?

What does your hairstyle say
about you?

· ·

 What is your favorite kids' game or
board game? Why is it so fun?

What character from a book would you like to come to life? How would you like to interact with that character?

 What is one fun family goal that you'd love to work on together for the next year? Why?

You're the parent for the day! What family rules would you get rid of for good? Why?

 What's the best part of the weekend? What's your favorite way to spend time off work or school?

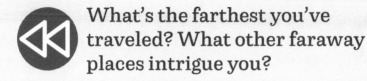 What's the farthest you've traveled? What other faraway places intrigue you?

 If you could only wear one color for the rest of your life, which would it be? If your whole family had to match, what color would you choose for all of you to wear?

When you were younger, what job or career did you dream of having? Has that dream changed?

 What does it take to make a family feel close to one another? How do you like to create close connections to the people in your family?

When do you most need alone time? What do you do when you get it?

 What food reminds you most of your grandparents or older loved ones? What stories or feelings does it evoke?

If you were five inches taller or five inches shorter, what might change about your daily life? What would be challenging or exciting about being a different height?

 If you were a doctor, what would your specialty be, and why?

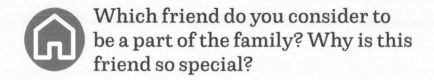 Which friend do you consider to be a part of the family? Why is this friend so special?

 What kind of art inspires you? How does it light you up?

Have you ever been scared of an animal? What made you feel afraid?

 What are your go-to road-trip snacks? What snacks would you buy for each of your family members?

What is a bad habit you've successfully stopped? How did you break the habit? Who helped you?

 What's one thing you'd like your family to get better at doing together? How might things change if you were better at that thing?

What's the best thank-you that you've ever received? Why did it mean so much?

 When was a time you felt shy around other people? How do you handle your moments of shyness? What or who helps you embrace your shy times or move through them?

Your family has joined the circus! What act will you all perform to really wow the audience? Why would your family dazzle during this act?

What is one terrible job that you'd agree to do for a full year if it paid a million dollars? What or who would help you make it through until the big payday?

What should you be in charge of in your family? What is something you should definitely *not* be the boss of in your family?

 Which athlete is a great role model for kids? Why are they inspiring for younger generations?

What did you think about blended families before you became a part of one? If someone asked you to define a blended family today, what would you say?

 What brand-new school or office supplies give you a thrill? Why do you enjoy them so much?

What kind of volunteering would you love to do? How might it help others and also be fulfilling for you? What are some ways your family could volunteer together?

 Why were you given your name? Is there a story or meaning behind it?

What act of kindness by a neighbor
has meant a lot to you and why?

 What's the best birthday you've
celebrated so far? What made
it special?

Imagine that it's family "yes" day—where every request is granted! If you get to skip work and school, what is the first fun activity your family should do together? What else would be on the agenda for this fun day, and why?

 What is one super-messy activity you love to do? How does it feel to be messy in that moment?

How does your family resolve
conflicts or solve problems?

 What kind of surprises are *not* fun
for you? Why?

Have you ever had a crush on someone? What made them special?

 What song do you like to belt out in the shower? What songs do your family members sing behind closed bathroom doors?

Which book do you wish you'd written, and why? Is there anything you'd rewrite if you were the author?

 What is one thing you'd change about the city or town where you live? What's something you love about your hometown?

Is it okay to gossip? How do you usually react when you hear gossip?

 What was a moment when you felt really free? When you envision that moment, what details come to mind?

When you open up a goody bag from a party, what do you hope will be inside? What's something you hope will not be in it?

 What is a problem in the world you know you could fix if you only had more time and money? Why are you the right person to come up with the best solution?

What does your family enjoy doing outside together? What outdoor activities do you think would be fun to try as a family?

 Which sport do you love to watch but have no interest in playing? Why are you best suited to be a fan cheering in the stands, on the sideline, or from home?

When did you first learn about marriage and divorce? What messages from movies or friends or your family have stuck with you about marriage and divorce?

If your family was competing in a cooking challenge on a reality show, what meal would you make together? How would you help whip up the winning dish?

Do you think high schoolers should work after school? How do you think this might help or hurt them now, or after graduation?

 What's the coziest spot in your home? How do you enjoy that space?

If a friend hurts your feelings, how do you tell them? How do you want them to tell you if you hurt their feelings?

Have you ever cheated at a game? Be honest! What happened?

Your family has just arrived at a vacation rental home, and you get the first pick of the top bunk bed or the bottom. Which is the best, and why?

What topic could you write a book on or give a speech about today without any preparation? How did you develop that expertise?

What is okay to share on social media about your family? What would you like to make a pact to never share there?

 Do you believe in reincarnation? What might you have been like or accomplished in a previous life?

When is a time you got away with breaking the rules? What happened, and how do you feel about that choice now?

 What playground games or activities are the most fun for you? Who do you enjoy playing with at the park?

When you envision where you will live in 10 years, what comes to mind? Will it be in a different home or city? Who will be with you?

 Which holiday do you love celebrating most with your family, and why?

What's a fear you've overcome?
How did you overcome it?

 Your family is creating a time
capsule of this year! What are three
items you will put into it to archive
the year? What do you predict your
other family members will add?

What's the funniest award or honor you've ever been given? What hilarious trophy would you like to win?

 If you could take a family trip to one of the current Seven Wonders of the World—for example, the Great Wall of China, the Chichen Itza pyramid in Mexico, or the Taj Mahal in India—which would you choose, and why?

What do you think is the biggest challenge of living with other people (waiting in line for the bathroom, so little quiet time, all the snoring from the other room, or something else)?

 What word do you say way too often? What word could you use to replace it? How long do you think you can go without saying it?

Have you ever been in an ambulance, emergency room, or hospital? If so, how did it feel to be there, and how did it feel to go home? If not, what do you imagine it's like?

 What's the most delicious food on a kids' menu? What food would you add to a children's menu?

What is the world record that only you could break? Is it for something serious or silly that you can do?

 How is your family different from other families? How is this challenging? How is this wonderful?

How do you like to share the experience of reading a book with someone else? Do you like to participate in a book club, have someone read aloud to you, or share your favorite passages with someone?

Who was your first friend? What do you remember about them?

Would you prefer to have your portrait painted by a famous artist to hang in a museum, a song written about you to play on the radio, or a poem composed about you that's in a prizewinning book? Why? How would this honor feel?

 Where in nature are you the most inspired to be creative?

In what ways can a parent who might not have given birth to their children or may still be getting to know kids in their family show them that they really care? In what ways do you show your love to your blended family?

 If you could save any three animals from extinction, which would you protect, and why?

Have you ever seen someone do something you knew was wrong? How did it feel to witness that? What did you do?

 If you could bake a cake for anyone in your family, what flavors and decorations would you choose that you know they'd love?

Which movie or book character would you like to be your friend? Why do you think they'd make a good friend?

 What would you like to know about your family history? How could you find out more information about your family?

What do people assume about you because of the place where you live? Are they correct?

 When was the best day of your life? What made it so amazing?

Technical difficulty! Laptop, tablet, phone, remote doorbell, gaming console—you can only keep one tech device. Which do you choose, and why?

What's the biggest dream you have for yourself right now? What do you imagine it would feel like to make it happen? How can your family help?

If you are standing at the podium accepting an award or championship ring or other great honor, what would you say to thank your family for helping you get there?

 What's something wonderfully quirky or weird about you? How do you embrace this about yourself?

How did you learn about death? What would you like to know? What do you think is important for other people to understand about death and dying?

You get to go glamping—camping in luxury and comfort! What three extravagant items would you set up in your tent? How would these items take your camping trip up a notch?

What is something you are naturally good at that other people have to spend time working hard on or practicing? How do you use that talent?

 When do you miss members of your family? How do you stay connected when you're apart? What helps ease those feelings?

How do you keep yourself entertained when you are bored at school or work?

What is something big that happened in your life that you can't remember at all and only know about through photos or stories? Do you wish you remembered it?

You've been voted the leader of a brand-new country! What do you name this country? And what is the first law you put into place?

 If you won an all-expenses-paid vacation anywhere in the world, where would you take your family? What would you do while you're there?

What words of wisdom have you received about being a part of a blended family? How has that guidance held up?

 When was the last time you felt scared? How did you get through that moment and past that feeling? What helps you feel reassured and calm when you are frightened?

When has someone misjudged you? What did that person get wrong about you?

 You've just won your dream car or vehicle. What will you be driving, and why is it your dream?

What is one small thing you do that has a positive impact on your community, city, or the world? What inspires you to do it?

 What's something your family did or does that might surprise other people but is no big deal to you (for example, dive into a snowbank while wearing swimsuits, go to bed right after dinner, or put ketchup on mac and cheese)?

When you're feeling sad or cranky, which person outside the family can always cheer you up? How do they help turn your feelings around?

What team, club, or group have you loved being a member of, and why?

What is a lunch you could eat every single day and always enjoy?

· ·

What is something you would like to change about your life so that you feel healthier and happier? What will it take to make this change?

Where does your family gather for meals? If you were in charge of switching it up, where would you change the location to?

 What's something you've forgiven yourself for? Did anything change after that for you?

What is the most bored you've ever been? How did you manage?

 What song gets stuck in your head? How do you get rid of that earworm?

Imagine yourself 20 years from now. What advice would future you give to the present-day you? What would you want to know from future you?

 What's something you have to share at home that you'd really like to be just for you? If you had to pitch making that thing only yours, what would you say?

What question would you like people to stop asking you? Why is this question off-limits?

 What is a fact or something you learned in school that is still stuck in your head? Why do you think you still remember it?

What mythical animal would you like to have as a family pet, and why?

 What's the best way to spend the first day of summer break? What do you look forward to when the weather is warm and sunny?

If you had to make up a nonsense word to describe your family, what silly word would it be? What is the meaning of this made-up word? How would you use it in a sentence about your family?

 What movie, scene from a show, or commercial always makes you cry? Why does it spark such an emotional response?

Which friend or loved one would you really like to reconnect with or spend more time with soon? When was the last time you were with them?

 If you climbed to the summit of the tallest mountain in the world, what would you yell out to the world below? What might your family members yell out?

Who do enjoy eating lunch with while at work or school? Why is this person your lunch buddy? If you don't have a lunch buddy, do you enjoy talking to others while eating or eating silently?

 Which room in your home would you most like to remodel or redecorate? What do you dream that space would look like after the big reveal?

If a handwritten letter arrived in the mail addressed to you, who would you hope it was from? What do you hope it would say?

 If you could rewrite one memory from the last year, what would you change? Would you say something funny or express how you were really feeling? Would you change the people who were there or invite someone new into that memory? Would you change what happened?

If you could be cast in any TV or YouTube show, which show would you want to appear on? Why would you be a good fit for it?

 What is a class or grade in school you'd actually have fun taking again? Why would you choose this school do-over?

What's your favorite way that your family is active together? When was the last time you enjoyed that activity?

· ·

 What favorite thing or activity would you be willing to give up completely in order to live 10 extra years?

What national or world event has impacted your life? How did it change you or the way you live?

 What theme song should play when you enter a room? (Bonus points for showing your family how you'd make your entrance with that song blasting!)

How have you helped someone else accomplish a goal or do something really great? How was it to be a part of the process?

 If you could teach someone in your family to play a sport or do an activity that you love so they enjoy it with you, who would you pick and what would you teach them? Who else would you invite to participate?

If you could delete one subject in school for all students, for all time, which subject would you erase, and why?

 Have you ever laughed at a really inappropriate time? (Can you tell the story without laughing now?)

 When are you at your silliest?
Who else in your family has
silly moments?

 What is something you've read or
heard that changed the way you
think? What did it shift for you?

What's the perfect pet for your family, in your opinion? What do you think the other people in your family would say?

 What color are the crayons that you rarely or never use? What are your favorite colors in the box? Which ones do you wear down first from using so often?

Have you ever had a mishap that you laughed about later? When has something gone really wrong but turned out to be totally fine (and even kind of funny) in the end?

 When you doodle, what do you usually draw? Why do you doodle it?

What's something you've always wanted to do but are not allowed to do?

 If your family had to completely change the way you communicate for 24 hours, what method would you choose? Would you opt for texting, writing notes, singing everything you want to say, or maybe using a different language?

What are some ways you take good care of your body? How do these routines help you feel better?

 What is one way a friendship has made you a better person? How did it change you?

Winner, winner, chicken dinner! Your family is awarded food from a favorite restaurant every week for the next year. What one restaurant do you choose? Which restaurant will your family members choose?

What totally useless skill or ridiculous talent do you love having? How or when do you share it?

How are you different when you're with your family than you are when you are with other people? Do you notice a difference in how your family members are at home and then with others?

 How do you react when someone gets in trouble at school or work? What do you think or feel when you witness those situations? How do other people around you respond?

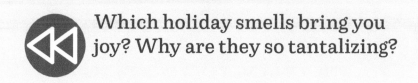 Which holiday smells bring you joy? Why are they so tantalizing?

 If you were competing in a gaming world championship, what game would you play to take home the blue ribbon? Would you choose a video game, board game, or something else?

Imagine yourself in 10 years. What will you look like? Where will you live? What will you be doing?

 If being a blended family makes you superheroes, what is your own special power to help out your family and other families like yours?

What is a sound you love? What's a sound you can't stand? What happens when you hear it?

Have you ever offered assistance to a new student or coworker or teammate who needed help? What happened?

If cell phones suddenly disappeared, what would be the biggest challenge for you? The best part?

 What are some of your concerns about the future, and why? Who or what could help soothe or resolve these concerns?

What special quality do you bring to your family (for example, a sense of humor, hugs, supporting others, or some other unique characteristic)? What special qualities do each of your family members contribute?

 What's one regret you have? How did you make peace with it?

What's something you do simply because it reminds you of a parent, grandparent, or someone older you love? How does this ritual help connect you to that loved one or their memory?

 If you were in charge of creating the menu for a holiday or special occasion, what food would you include? Would you switch up the menu from other years, or would you stick to your family favorites?

What goal have you been the proudest to reach? What strategies and which people helped you along the way?

When you are at the movies with your family, which snacks are you willing to share, and which ones do you keep to yourself? What treats do you like to eat when you have movie night at home?

If you had to get rid of one holiday from the calendar, which would you delete? Why would you choose that holiday? How would your family members react?

 Have you ever gotten lost or separated from your family? How did you find your way back?

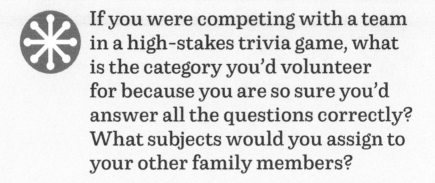 If you were competing with a team in a high-stakes trivia game, what is the category you'd volunteer for because you are so sure you'd answer all the questions correctly? What subjects would you assign to your other family members?

 What's a natural talent you would love to have? Why?

When has a hug or kiss from a parent or other trusted family member made everything better for you?

 What's something that makes you instantly angry or want to yell? What's something that makes the other people in your family that mad?

What's something spontaneous you've done that turned out to be fun? Why was it such a blast?

 If you met someone who'd never watched TV before and wanted to get caught up, what are three of the greatest shows that you'd recommend to them? What are a few shows your family members would add to the list?

When you want to give up on something, how do you keep going? What have you learned from persevering when you want to quit?

 If your family was adding one more room to the house, how would you vote for the room to be used? What if the room had to be open for everyone in the family to use?

Which season do you look forward to the most? What are the top three things you love most about that time of year?

 Have you ever been sent to the principal's office or gotten in trouble with your boss? How did it feel?

Which food that you hate would you be willing to try again? What would entice you to give it another try?

What is a job you dream of having but definitely do not have the skills or talent to do (for now)? What would it be like to have that dream job?

If family hugs and snuggles were a color, what color would they be? Why did you choose that color?

What do you need to take a great nap? Does it need to be dark and silent, or can you fall asleep in any crowded, noisy room? Do you like white noise or maybe your favorite blankie to sleep well?

What is your favorite way to pass the time on a long car or bus ride? Do you prefer to play games, listen to podcasts, sleep, or do something else to make the most of your trip?

 If you turned into a sea creature tomorrow, which one would you want to become for the day? Why?

What is a skill you'd like to improve? How committed are you to practicing in order to get better?

Which Disney character is most like you? Which characters are most like the rest of your family members? What Disney movie would be the perfect place for your family of characters?

What's the best breakfast of all time? What makes this food so delicious to you? Would the others in your family agree?

 When you were growing up or before you had children, what kind of parent did you think you'd be? If you are a kid, what kind of parent can you imagine yourself being?

If movies, television, streaming, and gaming are turned off for a year, what new hobby or activity would you do during that time? How else could you make the most of a screen-time shutdown?

 Give yourself a pat on the back! What is an accomplishment at work or school you are super proud of achieving?

If your family became tourists in your own town, what local place would you love to visit that you haven't been to yet? Why do you want to go there?

 Would you ever want to run for office? What elected position would you like to hold? (Bonus points if you come up with a catchy campaign slogan!)

Think back to your first day at school, work, on a team, or volunteering somewhere new. What was it like for you? What was the biggest challenge? Were there any happy surprises?

How do you describe your clothing style? If you were in a fashion show wearing your favorite outfits, what would the title of your collection be?

If you could spend a summer touring the country seeing any singer, band, or musician, whose shows would you love to see night after night? Why would you choose this tour?

 What's one space in your home you really like to keep clean and tidy? What's your strategy to keep it in order? Do other people in your family help keep it neat, or is this your choice or responsibility?

Who has stepped up to be a wonderful friend to you when you least expected it? In what ways have they been there for you?

What's something spooky you've witnessed or heard? Why was it so creepy?

Ahoy! If you were setting off to sail around the world, who are the two crew members you'd choose to assist you? What special skills or traits will they bring to this boating adventure?

To which author would you like to write a letter to share your thoughts about their books and what their work means to you? How would you start the letter?

How do other people describe your family? What is accurate, and which descriptions are not exactly true?

 What is something you are a real nerd about, and why? Do other people know that you nerd out on this, or is it something you keep to yourself?

What's a food you used to love to eat but can no longer stomach? When and why did your taste change?

 Jungle, forest, a beach, or somewhere else in nature—where would you choose to live outdoors, and what would it be like to live there?

How would you feel about living on the road and traveling by RV, van, or car? How might that life fill you with joy? And what might be the challenges?

· ·

 How important is it to be on time in your family? Are the people in your family planners who prepare things in advance, or are you all more spontaneous and flexible?

What is the best idea you've ever had? What made it so brilliant?

 When is a time you worked really hard on something and put in a lot of effort, time, and thought? Did you get the recognition or acknowledgment you expected? What did that experience teach you?

If you were a professional artist, what kind of art would you create? Where would you like your artwork to be displayed?

Where do you do your best work? Where do you need to be so you are focused, productive, or creative? How do you like to sit, and what do you need around you?

How are you similar to each of your parents? What's one way you're really different?

 Who makes you laugh the hardest? And who do you make laugh the most?

Who taught you how to cook? Or who would you like to teach you how to cook? What did you learn, or what would you like to learn to make?

Your family can only watch one movie for the next year. What movie do you choose for the whole family to watch (over and over!)? What would your other family members choose?

What luxuries do you enjoy? What fancy, frivolous, or fun things, activities, or services would you always like to make room for in the budget?

What's your favorite way to fall asleep? What bedtime routines help you wind down from your day? What new routines would you like to add? Which ones are you ready to delete?

What kind of music really lights you up? Does your family share your love of this kind of music?

 What would you like your legacy to be? What do you hope future generations of your family remember or pass on about you? What stories do you hope they tell about your life?

If someone sent you a big bouquet of flowers as a surprise just for being amazing you, which flowers would you like them to include? Why?

 If you could make a wish come true for one of your family members, who would it be and what wish would you choose? If you could make a wish for your whole family, what would it be?

Looking Back

You made it to the end! That doesn't mean it is over. This is the perfect time to look back on what you learned about each other (and yourself).

What you have created in this book is far more than a bunch of responses to questions. You have shared small moments, plot twists, and full chapters of your stories. You've dreamed aloud together and set goals for tomorrow, next year, and your big, beautiful futures, individually and together. Hopefully, in these moments you witnessed the power of family to cheer each other on in the triumphs, support each other as we do big things, and hold on to each other when our feelings and lives feel big. As a blended family, you are choosing to be there with one another during it all, and while that is not always easy, it is certainly magnificent.

So, what's next?

Flip through the pages and reread your responses, if you chose to write them down, or simply reminisce about them. Think about which questions were the most challenging to you, and which ones ignited the most laughs. Reflect on the honest answers that were hard but important to hear. Talk to each other about the questions that have stayed with you, and if there are any you'd like to add to this book or delete from it. Which of the 400 questions would you like to be asked again? Most importantly, what did you love about spending this time together? And how will you keep the magic going?

Acknowledgments

A thousand thank-yous:

To blended families, and those going through big transitions at home. You are writing new and beautiful definitions of what it means to be a loving family and showing us all how to grow, connect, and change together.

To my children, Ethan and Grace, for filling our home with your own soulful questions and insights, laughter, kitchen dance parties, and reminders that I'm the funniest in this family. To my parents and the Ashleys, for being right there during all of our family transitions and celebrations.

And to my advisory board of brilliant moms and women (especially my fempire) who generously give advice, grace, and reminders that it'll all be okay in the end (if it's not okay, it's not the end).

About the Author

Jessica Ashley is an award-winning writer and certified divorce coach at Divorce Coach for Moms. She's the voice of Single Mom Nation and its sister podcast and an instructor at Northwestern University with three independently published books. She answers to both Jessica and Ashley. Connect with Jessica at DivorceCoachforMoms.com or Jessica-Ashley.com.